#1 SECRET TO DENTAL SEO

"EXPERTS" DON'T WANT YOU TO KNOW EXPOSED!

#1 SECRET TO DENTAL SEO
"EXPERTS" DON'T WANT YOU TO KNOW EXPOSED!

Chad Levin

#1 Secret To Dental SEO "Experts" Don't Want You To Know Exposed!

Visit the authors website at 7DigitDentalMarketing.com

Published & Distributed by Chad Levin 4023 Kennett Pike #50364, Wilmington, DE 19807

Rights & Permissions and For information about special discounts available for bulk purchases, sales promotions, fund-raising, and educational needs, contact: Chad Levin, 4023 KENNETT PIKE, #50364, WILMINGTON, DE, 19807, United States, chad@7DigitDentalMarketing.com

Printed in the United States of America Second Edition 2024
Cover Design & Interior Design: Olga Pomazanova

Please note: The practice of search engine optimization (SEO) is constantly evolving. Search engine companies independently develop and update their own algorithms for generating search engine results. The information presented in this book is not intended to manipulate search engine companies, search engine algorithms, search engine terms of service, or search engine quality guidelines. The creators and publishers of this book disclaim any liabilities or loss in connection with following any strategies described in this book, and implementation is at the discretion, decision and risk of the reader.

ePub ISBN: 979-8-9888316-4-8
PDF ISBN: 979-8-9888316-5-5
Paperback ISBN: 979-8-9888316-3-1

Contents

CHAPTER 1:

No More Nonsense

You have been called & emailed by thousands of "Dental SEO experts" claiming they can get your dental practice website to page one on google. Maybe you purchased their services and did not get the results you expected. We have all been there.

The overall goal is to increase patients visiting your website by ensuring that your website appears highest in rank on search engine results pages like google, bing, and yahoo.

The reason you did not get the results you expected is because the Dental SEO agency did not have the one resource required to get you the results you expected.

I am going to tell you exactly what that one resource is today. It works for any dental practice website.

CHAPTER 2:

Why It Works

Why it works is because it is the same as giving referrals. For example, let's suppose you are a dentist in Miami and a client contacts you for dental services in Chicago, which is hundreds of miles away. You, as a Miami dentist, are not going to travel to Chicago to service one client as it would not be profitable due to the cost of travel. You are going to refer the dental services request to a dental office in the city they are calling from, which in this example is Chicago.

Imagine that the client was able to visit the Chicago dentist website you referred them to directly from your Miami dentist website as an instant referral without ever calling you. Do you see the value in that? You should because the top search engines in the world do.

Google, bing and yahoo value referrals so much that it is the highest graded factor for ranking websites in their search engine results pages that billions of people use every day. This is how the search engine algorithms have worked since they were created and this strategy will survive through any google update.

CHAPTER 3:

How I Learned That This Strategy Works

Many years ago I owned a national health insurance brokerage website and hired many SEO agencies. None of them helped me. They only took my money. Finally through trial and error, I taught myself how to do SEO and my health insurance website ranked on page one of google for top keyword phrases such as "health insurance quotes" and "individual health insurance" above the top competitors such as blue cross blue shield, united health care and many more using the exact same strategy in this book. The company became the fourth largest online individual health insurance brokerage in the U.S.A in one year as leads poured in from people finding my website on google from searching thousands of different keywords.

I sold the company during the U.S. Healthcare Reform Act because commissions were cut drastically and it did not pay to be in the individual health insurance business any longer.

After selling the insurance company I opened a dental digital marketing agency and serviced thousands of dentists around the world for SEO. Over ninety-nine percent of those dental websites I serviced achieved page one rankings on google, bing, and yahoo using this same strategy explained in this book. Competitors have tried to copy my techniques or say that I have worked at their SEO agency, with no validity.

The secret to Dental SEO is revealed in the next section. I wish you the best of luck in your campaigns.

CHAPTER 4:

The Secret Resource to SEO Revealed

The truth is that the secret to Dental SEO is no secret at all. Every Dental SEO expert knows exactly what is needed to make your website number one on the search engines. The problem is that they don't have that one resource available to them and that one resource is very hard to get. As the saying goes, if it were easy then everyone would be doing it.

The term for this resource is a term you have heard before. You must fully understand that there is one specific type that holds the most value. There are many different types and each type has different values according to the search engines algorithms.

The resource that will bring the highest value to your website and get you to page one rankings fast is "industry links" from real business websites. An industry link from a real business website has 2 distinct characteristics:

1. It is a real business website.

2. 2. The real business website is in the same industry as the website you are promoting.

Going back to our example, I mentioned two dental practice websites for a reason. These websites are both in the same industry, dentistry. They are both real business websites. Two absolutely necessary characteristics in this equation. Therefore, if you have a dental practice website then you need other dental practice websites to link to your website. When those "industry links" are published on the other dental practice websites, the search engines will find them and your website will sky rocket to page one of the search engines within 30 to 90 days. This is due to the fact that search engines place the highest value on "industry links" from real business websites for ranking websites on their search results pages. This is how the search engines have worked since they were created and this strategy will survive through any google update.

Every single link that refers to your website is valued differently and that value comes from the source where the link is published. To help you understand this, I have provided a grading scale with examples from highest to lowest grade in the next chapter.

CHAPTER 5:

Source Grading Scale with Examples

(Listed Highest to Lowest)

1. "Industry links" from real business websites –

Gives the highest grade to your website due to relevance, which overpowers any other factors such as authority and trust. It must be a real business website only, not a blog or any other type of website, and it must be in the same industry.

Example – a dental practice website links to another dental practice website..

2. Editorial and press release links –

Gives a high grade to your website due to the power of the website the link is published on. Each individual website is graded by authority and trust, which is associated with the power of a website. "Industry links" from real business websites over power any type of authority or trust a website has due to relevance.

Example – pr.com or forbes.com publishes an article on their website that has a link to your website.

3. Website links from blogs or irrelevant websites –

Gives a mild grade due to a link being published. This can help or hurt depending upon the relevance of the website where the link is published.

Example – A food blog pinchofyum.com publishes an article on their website that has a link to a dental practice website.

4. Citation links –

Gives a mild grade due to a link being published. It lists your business name, address, phone number, and website.

Example – Business website information is published on a site like yelp.com

5. Social Media links –

Gives a mild grade due to a link being published. This is mainly used to get the search engines to visit your website and see new content. Because social media has a lot of website traffic, the search engines are constantly visiting and following these links. This is because search engines love new content.

Example – Website link is published on facebook.com or twitter.com

6. Directory links –

Gives a low grade due to a link being published. Google downgraded directory links many years ago as they were being used for spam purposes.

Disclaimer, citation links do come from directory types of websites and are treated differently by the search engines due to their trust and authority.

EExample – website link is published in craigslist.com

7. Private blog network –

Gives a fraudulent grade due to a link being published on a fraudulent website only being used to manipulate search engine rankings. This is a very dangerous strategy, a black hat strategy that can get your website banned from the search engines.

Example – Website link published on a restored website that is a fake business or blog.

There are thousands of different types of links that can be published on billions of websites. The fact remains, that strong "industry links" from real business websites receive the highest grade from the search engines. Therefore, pushing your website up the search engine rankings faster and safer than any other strategy.

The question is, how and where will you get your "industry links" from other dental practice websites? It's not easy! We will explore acquisition strategies in the next chapter.

CHAPTER 6:

Secret Resource Acquisition Strategies

1. **Manual** –

   Call or email dental practice owners and ask them for a link.

2. **Hire Link Outreach Services** –

   Hire a link outreach service to do the manual work for you.

3. **Ask An SEO Agency** –

   Not all Dental SEO agencies are bad. Some actually do the hard work for you to acquire "industry links" from dental practice websites.

Free Gift #1 BONUS:
Dental SEO Agency Interview Checklist

When interviewing Dental SEO agencies, your first question should be: "How are you going to acquire industry links from other dental practice websites?" If they cannot answer this question directly, then it is not the right agency to work with because they will not deliver the results you require.

Go to 7DigitDental.com/seo Select **"Agency"** and download the **Free Dental SEO Agency Interview Checklist** to find additional questions to ask an SEO agency during an interview.

You can also scan the QR Code if you don't like typing.

CHAPTER 7:

How Many Secret Resources Do I Need?

You won't need many secret resources due to the power of each "industry link." Start with getting five dental practice websites to agree to link to your dental practice website. In the link text, use the same keyword phrase on all five websites.

An example of a keyword phrase for a local dentist would be "dentist chicago il". Wait 30 to 90 days to see where you are ranking in the search engines for the exact keyword phrase compared to where you were ranking when you started. Add 5 more links from 5 new dental websites every 30 to 90 days until you reach your goal.

I usually like to start with 5 keyword phrases and a total of 25 "industry links" from dental practice websites. You can use the google keyword planner to figure out your keyword phrases.

Be very specific when choosing your final keyword phrases. For example, if I were going to promote a dentist in Chicago Illinois, I would choose the following top 5 keyword phrases below:

Dentist Chicago IL
Dentists Chicago IL
Dentist Office Chicago IL
Family Dentist Chicago IL
Cosmetic Dentist Chicago

Free Gift #2 BONUS:
Use Keywords I Personally Use

Save time and find the best performing keywords for Dental SEO.

Go To 7DigitDental.com/seo and select **"Google Keyword Planner"** to download the **Free Bonus Keyword List** that I personally use when creating Dental SEO campaigns for clients. You can use it for your dental practice to get new patients fast. This one is on me!

You can also scan the QR Code if you don't like typing..

CHAPTER 8:

How to Structure Secret Resources

When structuring an "industry link", you will use the same text as your keyword phrase target.

Example – keyword phrase target is "dentist chicago il." Then the text in the link, also known as anchor text will also be exactly the same "dentist chicago il."

The link will go to the dentist chicago il page on your website and/or your home page. Follow instructions in Chapter 10 on how to easily create the page on your website to tie this all together.

CHAPTER 9:

When will I See Results?

(Be Realistic)

You will see rankings increase in the first 30 days from their current positions. We all wish the results of being on the first page will come instantly and with this strategy they will happen faster than any other Dental SEO strategy. Local results come much faster than national results. Keep this in mind when planning your campaign. If the website you are promoting has no rankings now, then start with a local campaign. As the old saying goes "crawl before you walk." The same applies here. After working with thousands of dental websites over the years, I can give you averages that will help you gauge success. The averages below are how long it will take to reach the first page.

Local campaigns –

30 to 90 days on average; for example keyword "dentist chicago il".

National campaigns –

3 months to 6 months on average; for example keyword "dentist". National campaigns are more difficult and can sometimes take up to one year.

CHAPTER 10:

How to Structure Website Pages for Success

Everything we discussed previously is part of the off page seo. SEO has two parts; off page seo, which is not on the website and on page seo which is on the website. On page seo establishes the foundation of your SEO campaign, acting as the engine in a car. Off page seo serves as the gasoline that powers your engine, making it work effectively.

I am going to show you exactly what to do for on page seo in a few steps to assemble this all together and provide you with a live example at the end of this chapter.

When you are creating a page on your dental practice website, you want to be as exact as possible so the search engines can easily understand what you want to rank for. Let's say we are making a page that we want to rank on the search engines for the keyword phrase "dentist chicago il." Below is how the page should be structured for best SEO performance.

URL – yourwebsite.com/dentist-chicago-il (always use lowercase for url)

Page Title / Meta Title – Dentist Chicago IL

Page Description / Meta Description – Dentist Chicago IL

Content/ Text on page –
Create 500 words of unique text (not duplicated) on the page with "dentist chicago il" in the first paragraph. Link "dentist chicago il" found in the first paragraph to your home page (example yourweb-site.com). Add "dentist chicago il" two more times in the text. In total there should be three mentions of "dentist chicago il" in the text.

Silo –
At the bottom of the page, link to the other pages you want to rank. This is called a silo. For example, when promoting a dentist in chicago for five key-word phrases I would have the following **list of links at the bottom of each page in the silo** created for this campaign:

Link Text – dentist chicago il
Link URL – yourwebsite.com/dentist-chicago-il

Link Text – dentists chicago il
Link URL – yourwebsite.com/dentists-chicago-il

Link Text – dentist office chicago il
Link URL – yourwebsite.com/dentist-office-chicago-il

Link Text – family dentist chicago il

Link URL – yourwebsite.com/
famiy-dentist-chicago-il

Link Text – cosmetic dentist chicago il
Link URL – yourwebsite.com/
cosmetic-dentist-chicago-il

Free Gift #3 BONUS:
Create a Winning SEO Page with Me

Website SEO pages can make or break your rankings. They are like dynamite, they can be incredibly powerful if in the hands of an expert.

Go to 7DigitDental.com/seo Select **"Website Pages"** to watch a short video tutorial so you can start using this in your business to make more sales ASAP. I also made a **Free Website Pages Checklist** for you to use when creating pages on your website.

You can also scan the QR Code if you don't like typing. As always, it's absolutely free. Enjoy.

CHAPTER 11:

Trickle Down Theory Using Top Keywords

The trickle down theory is actually an economics term. Here we are using it in regards to Dental SEO and how search engines work.

You may be thinking, "Am I going to have to build links forever in order to get first page rankings for all of my keywords"? The answer is no. There are several answers to justify this and I will answer them one by one.

1. Using a phrase in the text of a link targets many variations of keyword searches. For example, using the text "dentist office chicago il" targets the following searches listed below:

    dentist office chicago il
    dentist office chicago
    dentist office (when a person living in the chicago area performs a search)
    dentist chicago il
    dentist chicago
    dentist (when a person living in the chicago area performs a search)

2. By targeting top keyword phrases, your website will also be found for many other dental keyword phrases that patients are searching for Website visits from your target keyword phrases being found on the search engines and the amount of time a visitor spends on your website are all search engine ranking factors. With an increase in both of these factors, your website will rank for more dental keyword phrases due to how the search engines algorithms work.

When visitors find your website to be relevant to their needs and spend more time on the website, search engines reward your website by ranking you for more keyword phrases. The job of search engines is to provide the most relevant results and new patients are finding your dental practice website to be relevant to their search.

3. By creating "industry links" from other dental practice websites, you are also creating a more powerful website. Your website will now be able to rank easier because it is more powerful than your competitors. Building more pages by following my directions in Chapter 10 "How to Structure Website & Pages for Success" will also increase the amount of keyword phrases your website will be found for substantially.

CHAPTER 12:

What Other Ranking Factors are Important?

In this book are the absolute most important and fastest strategies to achieve page one rankings for Dental SEO. In fact, there are over 200 ranking factors that influence search engines. Many we have already covered in this book. I will list some that will be of importance in achieving and maintaining your page one rankings:

1. **Domain Age** –

   The older the better. History builds trust with the search engines. More trust equals better rankings.

2. **Broken Links** –

   Make sure all links in your website are functioning and are not broken.

3. **Latent Semantic Indexing LSI** –

   Fancy term for adding keywords and synonyms of your keywords in the text of your website. Add keywords in the text and don't go overboard. Keep it simple.

4 **Website Speed** –

No one likes a slow website.

5. **Duplicate Content** –

Do not create duplicate text. All text must be unique and original. Do not have a duplicate website, choose to use the www or not and keep it that way by using the Rel=Canonical tag

---

Free Gift #4 BONUS:
Earn Google Trust Immediately

Don't let 200 google ranking factors affect your business. Go to 7DigitDental.com/seo and select **"Google Ranking Factors"** to ensure that your website is ready to skyrocket to number one on Google. Use the **Free Google Ranking Factors Checklist** I created for you.

You can also scan the QR Code if you don't like typing.

CHAPTER 13:

Increasing Conversions with SEO

Increasing conversions with SEO is fairly simple, this can be achieved by adding many calls to action. In our example of a dentist, the goal would be to generate new patient appointments. Adding the phone number in many places can certainly increase the amount of new patients coming from the website and SEO campaign. Below I will list some areas where a phone number can be added to generate more patients.

1. **Page Description / Meta Description** –

   Dentist Chicago IL (add phone number here)

2. **Website Header** –

   Add the phone number at the top of the website next to the navigation links usually in the top right position.

3. **Image** –

   Add the phone number above the fold (above the fold means before scrolling down)

4. **Content** –

   Add the phone number in the first paragraph.

CHAPTER 14:

Do It Yourself (DIY) or Done For You (DFY) Services?

You can choose to **Do It Yourself (DIY)** using the resources in this book and our online training.

Alternatively, **Done For You (DFY)** services provide the fastest results. Start with a free website SEO evaluation from a Dental SEO expert at 7 Digit Dental Marketing - a reliable, fast, & hard working agency to partner with.

Free Gift #5 BONUS:
Evaluate Your Website With An Expert

Save time and start seeing results. Together we can personally evaluate your dental practice website for free.

Go to 7DigitDental.com/seo Select **"Agency"** and download the **Free Dental SEO Evaluation Checklist** to get started. Then schedule a call with me at 7DigitDental.com or Call (888) 850-2137.

You can also scan the QR Codes if you don't like typing.

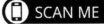

If you found this book helpful, I would greatly appreciate it if you could take a moment to leave a review on Google & Amazon. Your feedback means a lot to me!

Go to 7DigitDental.com/seo Select **"Reviews"** to find the **Review Links.**

You can also scan the QR Code if you don't like typing.

About the Author

Chad Levin

Founder & CEO of 7 Digit Dental Marketing

Dental SEO & Digital Marketing Strategist since 2007, dedicated to optimizing dental practice websites for first-page Google rankings. Specializing in attracting financially qualified patients, I drive tangible results for dental practices seeking growth.

7DigitDental.com

Follow us on social media: @7digitdentalmarketing

Made in United States
Orlando, FL
27 September 2024

52036529R00024